**Identically Different: It's An Oxymoron**

Copyright © Khalia Shalon Parker Preyer, 2020

Cover image: © Naafi Nur Rohma

ISBN : 978-1-7350896-2-1

Publisher's Note

Printed and bound in the United States of America. All rights reserved. No part of this book may be reproduced or transmitted in any form or by any means, electronic or mechanical, including photocopying, recording, or by any information storage and retrieval system except by a review who may quote brief passages in a review to be printed in a magazine, newspaper, or on the Web without permission in writing from Khalia Shalon Parker Preyer.

Although the author and publisher have made every effort to ensure the accuracy and completeness of information contained in this book, we assume no responsibility for errors, inaccuracies, omissions, or any inconsistency herein. The advice and strategies contained herein may not be suitable for your situation. You should consult with a professional where appropriate. Neither the publisher nor the author shall be liable for damages arising here from.

## Dedication

We are in a place of uncertainty in this day, this moment, and we are learning to love the beauty of simply being different. Jayce and Chance, you've inspired me to explore and value your being and differences though you were born on the same day. I hope this book will help you always remember my respect and love for you and challenge you to exhibit self-love. To my aunts Evelyn and Shirley, I appreciate your help and support through the challenge. Thank you both for getting this book in the hands of my readers. Leigh Ann, you are simply the best librarian ever; thanks for always being resourceful. Charles Albert, thanks for allowing me to ignite a NEW love for reading in you. It's a memory I will forever cherish. "Mommie," I hope my differences have somehow made you proud. This book is dedicated to everyone who recognizes differences and embraces them. The year 2020 has been an oxymoron for all of us; we are alone together!

Hello, my name is Asa, and my brother's name is Ace. We like to run and jump all over the place.

We like ice cream, chocolate, and peanut butter.
We have the same father and mother.

If you haven't guessed yet, Ace is my twin.
Let's say we're different before we begin.

**We are identically different, but it's all good.
It's an oxymoron like clearly misunderstood.**

I like cars and colors green and yellow.
Ace likes blue, but I'm more mellow.

We both like to run and play with superhero suits.
Yet we like different characters, and eat different fruits.

Ace likes mangos, grapes, and strawberries.
And I prefer oranges, apples, and cherries.

**We are identically different, but we love the same.
It's an oxymoron like dry rain.**

Ace was born a little while before me.
However, we arrived at the same delivery.

We wear different outfits to the airport.
We each have our favorite sport.

**We are identically different even when we rant;
It's an oxymoron like giant ants.**

Look at our eyes. Ace eyes turn green at times, and mine are brown.
They call us "twins" all over town.

We race sometimes, but most times I let him pass.
And at school, we're in a different class.

**We are identically different at the end of the night.
It's an oxymoron like dim light.**

An oxymoron is two or more side by side words with opposite meanings.
We find oxymorons in many books we're reading.

Our teacher taught me about how funny they are and how they are used.
He gave me a lot of examples to share with Ace because he was confused.

**We are identically different; he's quiet, and I'm loud.
It's an oxymoron like alone in a crowd.**

Twins are two different people whether they are identical or not. Some people identify them by a particular spot.

We have styles and different types of hair.
    We give double the love that no other can compare.

**We are identically different; there is no doubt.
It's an oxymoron like inside out.**

**THE END**

## About the Author

Khalia S. Preyer, also known as "K (P) 2", is a Drama Teacher and Creative Writer. She is a native of Hallandale Beach, Florida. Equipped with an undergraduate degree in Theatre Education from Florida A&M University, and a Masters of Education in Reading, Literature, and Literacy from Georgia State University. Khalia uses her love for her twin boys to educate them about their gifts and impact on the world.

She desires that this book is used as a tool and resource for children as they grow to learn the figure of speech and the beauty of the English language. You can write K (P) 2 to tell your story on www. Kp2writes.com or email her at kp2writes@gmail.com.

## About the Illustrator

Naafi is a children's book illustrator and lecturer in the Department of Visual Communication Design (DKV) at Institute of Sains and Technology Terpadu Surabaya (ISTTS), Indonesia. She has experience as an illustrator of children's books (over eight years) and has illustrated more than 70 children's books. You can contact her at Naafinurrohma@gmail.com.

Naafi has the principle that "**A dream is only a dream if we do nothing to make it happen** ".

Made in the USA
Coppell, TX
21 October 2021